Multiplication II

Multi-Digit and Regrouping

Author David Hudson
Editor Kathy Rogers

Table of Contents

 • P.O. Box 883 • Dana Point, CA 92629
www.edupressinc.com
ISBN 1-56472-138-8
Printed in USA

Multiplication Function Chart

Follow the steps below to learn the steps used in multiplication.

How to Multiply

1

Multiply ones by ones.

3 x 7 = 21

Carry the 2.

1000	100	10	1
		2	
		5	7
	x	4	3
			1

2

Multiply tens by ones.

3 x 5 = 15 + 2 = 17

1000	100	10	1
		2	
		5	7
	x	4	3
	1	7	1

3

Put a 0 in the ones column.

1000	100	10	1
		2	
		5	7
	x	4	3
	1	7	1
			0

4

Multiply ones by tens.

4 x 7 = 28

Carry the 2.

1000	100	10	1
		2 ~~2~~	
		5	7
	x	4	3
	1	7	1
		8	0

5

Multiply tens by tens.

4 x 5 = 20 + 2 = 22

1000	100	10	1
		2 ~~2~~	
		5	7
	x	4	3
	1	7	1
2	2	8	0

6

Add.

$$\begin{array}{r} 171 \\ +\underline{2280} \\ 2451 \end{array}$$

1000	100	10	1
		2 ~~2~~	
		5	7
	x	4	3
	1	7	1
2	2	8	0
2	4	5	1

Multiplication Tables

0 x 1 = 0	0 x 2 = 0	0 x 3 = 0	0 x 4 = 0
1 x 1 = 1	1 x 2 = 2	1 x 3 = 3	1 x 4 = 4
2 x 1 = 2	2 x 2 = 4	2 x 3 = 6	2 x 4 = 8
3 x 1 = 3	3 x 2 = 6	3 x 3 = 9	3 x 4 = 12
4 x 1 = 4	4 x 2 = 8	4 x 3 = 12	4 x 4 = 16
5 x 1 = 5	5 x 2 = 10	5 x 3 = 15	5 x 4 = 20
6 x 1 = 6	6 x 2 = 12	6 x 3 = 18	6 x 4 = 24
7 x 1 = 7	7 x 2 = 14	7 x 3 = 21	7 x 4 = 28
8 x 1 = 8	8 x 2 = 16	8 x 3 = 24	8 x 4 = 32
9 x 1 = 9	9 x 2 = 18	9 x 3 = 27	9 x 4 = 36
10 x 1 = 10	10 x 2 = 20	10 x 3 = 30	10 x 4 = 40
11 x 1 = 11	11 x 2 = 22	11 x 3 = 33	11 x 4 = 44
12 x 1 = 12	12 x 2 = 24	12 x 3 = 36	12 x 4 = 48
0 x 5 = 0	0 x 6 = 0	0 x 7 = 0	0 x 8 = 0
1 x 5 = 5	1 x 6 = 6	1 x 7 = 7	1 x 8 = 8
2 x 5 = 10	2 x 6 = 12	2 x 7 = 14	2 x 8 = 16
3 x 5 = 15	3 x 6 = 18	3 x 7 = 21	3 x 8 = 24
4 x 5 = 20	4 x 6 = 24	4 x 7 = 28	4 x 8 = 32
5 x 5 = 25	5 x 6 = 30	5 x 7 = 35	5 x 8 = 40
6 x 5 = 30	6 x 6 = 36	6 x 7 = 42	6 x 8 = 48
7 x 5 = 35	7 x 6 = 42	7 x 7 = 49	7 x 8 = 56
8 x 5 = 40	8 x 6 = 48	8 x 7 = 56	8 x 8 = 64
9 x 5 = 45	9 x 6 = 54	9 x 7 = 63	9 x 8 = 72
10 x 5 = 50	10 x 6 = 60	10 x 7 = 70	10 x 8 = 80
11 x 5 = 55	11 x 6 = 66	11 x 7 = 77	11 x 8 = 88
12 x 5 = 60	12 x 6 = 72	12 x 7 = 84	12 x 8 = 96
0 x 9 = 0	0 x 10 = 0	0 x 11 = 0	0 x 12 = 0
1 x 9 = 9	1 x 10 = 10	1 x 11 = 11	1 x 12 = 12
2 x 9 = 18	2 x 10 = 20	2 x 11 = 22	2 x 12 = 24
3 x 9 = 27	3 x 10 = 30	3 x 11 = 33	3 x 12 = 36
4 x 9 = 36	4 x 10 = 40	4 x 11 = 44	4 x 12 = 48
5 x 9 = 45	5 x 10 = 50	5 x 11 = 55	5 x 12 = 60
6 x 9 = 54	6 x 10 = 60	6 x 11 = 66	6 x 12 = 72
7 x 9 = 63	7 x 10 = 70	7 x 11 = 77	7 x 12 = 84
8 x 9 = 72	8 x 10 = 80	8 x 11 = 88	8 x 12 = 96
9 x 9 = 81	9 x 10 = 90	9 x 11 = 99	9 x 12 =108
10 x 9 = 90	10 x 10 =100	10 x 11 =110	10 x 12 =120
11 x 9 = 99	11 x 10 =110	11 x 11 =121	11 x 12 =132
12 x 9 =108	12 x 10 =120	12 x 11 =132	12 x 12 =144

Multiplication Practice

1 x2	2 x2	3 x0	0 x1	4 x3	2 x0
2 x3	6 x0	8 x4	1 x4	9 x0	4 x2
5 x0	2 x1	7 x4	4 x0	6 x4	0 x0
0 x3	6 x2	3 x2	3 x1	7 x0	5 x1
4 x1	9 x4	9 x1	1 x0	9 x3	9 x2
4 x4	8 x2	8 x3	2 x4	1 x1	5 x2
8 x0	3 x3	6 x1	3 x4	7 x1	6 x3
1 x3	5 x3	5 x4	8 x1	0 x2	7 x2
7 x3	0 x4				

Review
Multiplying by 5 thru 9

Multiplication Practice

9 x5	0 x5	8 x7	5 x9	2 x8	7 x6
3 x5	4 x9	4 x7	1 x8	4 x5	0 x8
3 x6	2 x7	1 x9	7 x5	9 x8	5 x8
9 x9	1 x7	6 x9	1 x5	0 x6	9 x7
5 x5	7 x7	3 x9	4 x6	5 x6	6 x8
8 x9	1 x6	3 x7	8 x8	5 x7	2 x9
0 x7	7 x8	0 x9	6 x6	4 x8	6 x5
7 x9	9 x6	8 x6	2 x6	3 x8	6 x7
2 x5	8 x5				

Pretest
Multiplying by 1 digit

Multiplication Practice

13 x 2	20 x 3	11 x 9	41 x 2	13 x 3
57 x 7	25 x 9	36 x 2	48 x 5	22 x 9
33 x 2	69 x 1	10 x 8	65 x 1	41 x 2
352 x 8	176 x 5	306 x 4	280 x 7	917 x 6
33 x 9	46 x 8	69 x 2	65 x 3	87 x 2
79 x 4	59 x 3	38 x 2	77 x 5	12 x 9
637 x 7	422 x 4	380 x 4	996 x 6	245 x 3
880 x 4	406 x 8	180 x 7	104 x 3	409 x 7

Pretest
Multiplying by 2 and 3 digits

Multiplication Practice

23 x 21	21 x 34	42 x 12	19 x 11
92 x 57	78 x 20	50 x 44	66 x 66
37 x 40	96 x 82	30 x 76	75 x 57
497 x 653	934 x 478	847 x 875	348 x 956
906 x 324	229 x 409	850 x 630	708 x 520

Multiplying
2 digits by 1 digit
No regrouping

Multiplication Practice

Example

$$\begin{array}{r} 32 \\ \times 3 \\ \hline \end{array}$$

Multiply ones by ones.

10	1
3	**2**
x	**3**
	6

Multiply tens by ones.

10	1
3	2
x	**3**
9	6

$$\begin{array}{r} 12 \\ \times 4 \\ \hline \end{array} \quad \begin{array}{r} 11 \\ \times 6 \\ \hline \end{array} \quad \begin{array}{r} 41 \\ \times 2 \\ \hline \end{array} \quad \begin{array}{r} 23 \\ \times 3 \\ \hline \end{array} \quad \begin{array}{r} 30 \\ \times 2 \\ \hline \end{array}$$

$$\begin{array}{r} 11 \\ \times 9 \\ \hline \end{array} \quad \begin{array}{r} 13 \\ \times 3 \\ \hline \end{array} \quad \begin{array}{r} 30 \\ \times 3 \\ \hline \end{array} \quad \begin{array}{r} 22 \\ \times 4 \\ \hline \end{array} \quad \begin{array}{r} 44 \\ \times 2 \\ \hline \end{array}$$

$$\begin{array}{r} 77 \\ \times 1 \\ \hline \end{array} \quad \begin{array}{r} 10 \\ \times 8 \\ \hline \end{array} \quad \begin{array}{r} 43 \\ \times 2 \\ \hline \end{array} \quad \begin{array}{r} 31 \\ \times 3 \\ \hline \end{array} \quad \begin{array}{r} 12 \\ \times 3 \\ \hline \end{array}$$

$$\begin{array}{r} 22 \\ \times 2 \\ \hline \end{array} \quad \begin{array}{r} 14 \\ \times 2 \\ \hline \end{array} \quad \begin{array}{r} 90 \\ \times 1 \\ \hline \end{array} \quad \begin{array}{r} 11 \\ \times 8 \\ \hline \end{array} \quad \begin{array}{r} 49 \\ \times 1 \\ \hline \end{array}$$

$$\begin{array}{r} 19 \\ \times 1 \\ \hline \end{array} \quad \begin{array}{r} 27 \\ \times 1 \\ \hline \end{array} \quad \begin{array}{r} 11 \\ \times 4 \\ \hline \end{array} \quad \begin{array}{r} 13 \\ \times 2 \\ \hline \end{array} \quad \begin{array}{r} 65 \\ \times 1 \\ \hline \end{array}$$

$$\begin{array}{r} 34 \\ \times 2 \\ \hline \end{array} \quad \begin{array}{r} 21 \\ \times 4 \\ \hline \end{array} \quad \begin{array}{r} 32 \\ \times 2 \\ \hline \end{array} \quad \begin{array}{r} 99 \\ \times 1 \\ \hline \end{array} \quad \begin{array}{r} 10 \\ \times 9 \\ \hline \end{array}$$

Multiplying
2 digits by 1 digit
No regrouping

Multiplication Practice

11 x 6	89 x 1	34 x 2	22 x 4	13 x 3
13 x 2	10 x 9	32 x 2	38 x 1	10 x 5
98 x 1	41 x 2	22 x 3	11 x 3	23 x 3
12 x 4	10 x 5	11 x 4	28 x 1	10 x 6
33 x 2	10 x 8	69 x 1	65 x 1	10 x 2
79 x 1	12 x 3	34 x 2	11 x 5	12 x 2
31 x 3	10 x 7	21 x 4	10 x 6	23 x 3
11 x 7	41 x 2	18 x 1	11 x 8	49 x 1

Multiplying
2 digits by 1 digit
Regrouping

Multiplication Practice

Example

	8 3
x	4

Multiply ones by ones.

4 x 3 = 12

Carry the 1.

100	10	1
	1	
	8	3
	x	4
		2

Multiply tens by ones.

4 x 8 = 32 + 1 = 33

100	10	1
	1	
	8	3
	x	4
3	3	2

13 x 4	18 x 6	46 x 2	29 x 3	16 x 4
22 x 9	25 x 3	64 x 3	75 x 5	76 x 9
27 x 5	99 x 8	43 x 6	44 x 4	82 x 5
19 x 5	14 x 6	93 x 4	63 x 8	49 x 7
18 x 4	27 x 5	35 x 4	15 x 9	12 x 8
34 x 6	27 x 3	38 x 2	99 x 2	82 x 9

Multiplying
2 digits by 1 digit
Regrouping

Multiplication Practice

19 x 6	89 x 3	34 x 5	88 x 8	13 x 9
67 x 7	15 x 9	36 x 2	38 x 5	22 x 9
98 x 7	44 x 8	27 x 4	84 x 6	25 x 3
52 x 8	16 x 5	36 x 4	28 x 7	17 x 6
33 x 9	46 x 8	69 x 2	65 x 3	87 x 2
79 x 4	59 x 3	38 x 2	77 x 5	12 x 9
37 x 7	46 x 4	38 x 4	99 x 6	24 x 3
88 x 4	46 x 8	18 x 7	14 x 3	49 x 7

Multiplying
3 digits by 1 digit
Regrouping

Multiplication Practice

Example

Multiply ones by ones.

4 x 3 = 12

Carry the 1.

1000	100	10	1
		1	
	3	8	**3**
		x	**4**
			2

Multiply tens by ones.

4 x 8 = 32 + 1 = 33

Carry the 3.

1000	100	10	1
	3	1	
	3	**8**	3
		x	**4**
		3	2

Multiply hundreds by ones.

4 x 3 = 12 + 3 = 15

1000	100	10	1
	3		
	3	8	3
		x	**4**
1	**5**	3	2

114 x 4	517 x 6	706 x 2	529 x 3	317 x 4
623 x 9	426 x 3	164 x 3	275 x 5	674 x 9
327 x 5	299 x 8	840 x 6	444 x 4	882 x 5
419 x 5	814 x 6	793 x 4	263 x 8	249 x 7
118 x 4	207 x 4	935 x 4	515 x 9	612 x 8
434 x 5	727 x 3	608 x 2	999 x 3	883 x 9

Multiplying
3 digits by 1 digit
Regrouping

Multiplication Practice

317 x 7	288 x 2	324 x 5	848 x 8	273 x 9
464 x 8	205 x 9	736 x 2	308 x 5	222 x 9
598 x 7	844 x 3	237 x 6	884 x 5	285 x 3
152 x 6	196 x 5	370 x 4	238 x 7	367 x 6
333 x 5	505 x 4	689 x 2	657 x 3	827 x 4
472 x 4	959 x 3	538 x 5	727 x 5	123 x 9
437 x 7	642 x 4	358 x 6	969 x 6	249 x 8
188 x 4	746 x 8	918 x 7	814 x 3	409 x 7

Multiplying
2 and 3 digits by 1 digit

Multiplication Practice

32 x 2	13 x 4	88 x 9	114 x 4	884 x 5
238 x 7	22 x 4	18 x 6	79 x 4	515 x 9
196 x 5	41 x 8	605 x 2	49 x 2	426 x 8
65 x 3	874 x 9	31 x 8	273 x 3	80 x 9
745 x 6	15 x 8	777 x 7	421 x 5	33 x 2
79 x 2	19 x 3	364 x 2	76 x 4	967 x 7
368 x 3	66 x 7	291 x 4	600 x 6	293 x 4
76 x 7	404 x 4	18 x 7	198 x 8	479 x 2

Multiplying
2 digits by 2 digits
No regrouping

Multiplication Practice

Example

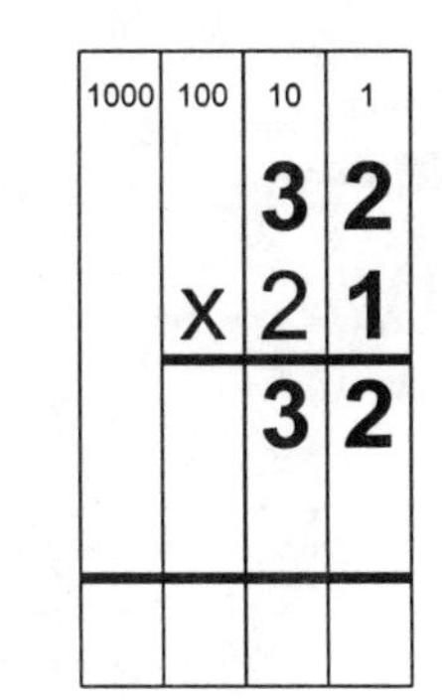

Multiply by ones.
1 x 32 = 32

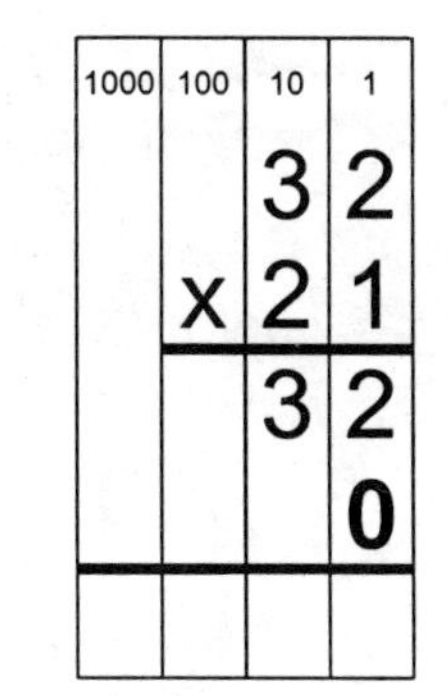

Put a zero in the ones column.

1000	100	10	1
		3	2
	x	2	1
		3	2
	6	4	0

Multiply by tens.
2 x 32 = 64

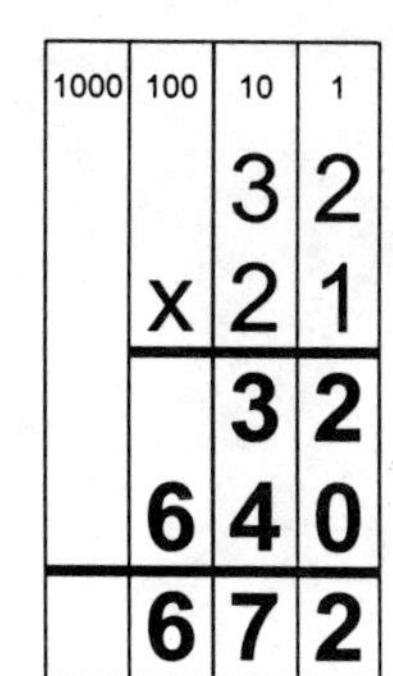

Add.
32 + 640 = 672

12 x 14 = 48 + 120	22 x 44 = 88 + 0	12 x 42 = 0	11 x 65	43 x 21
21 x 23	13 x 20	31 x 21	23 x 32	56 x 11
23 x 31	33 x 13	90 x 11	34 x 21	13 x 33

Multiplying
2 digits by 2 digits
No regrouping

Multiplication Practice

14 x 12	13 x 33	32 x 23	12 x 14	32 x 12
23 x 21	42 x 12	21 x 30	23 x 21	12 x 42
31 x 23	12 x 31	43 x 21	23 x 32	30 x 21
44 x 22	11 x 78	47 x 11	21 x 43	19 x 11
13 x 22	60 x 11	33 x 13	22 x 14	11 x 80

Multiplying
2 digits by 2 digits
Regrouping

Multiplication Practice

Example

Multiply ones by ones.

3 x 7 = 21

Carry the 2.

1000	100	10	1
		6 (carried 2)	7
	x	5	3
			1

Multiply tens by ones.

3 x 6 = 18 + 2 = 20

1000	100	10	1
		6 (carried 2)	7
	x	5	3
	2	0	1

Put a zero in the ones column.

1000	100	10	1
		6 (carried 2)	7
	x	5	3
	2	0	1
			0

Multiply ones by tens.

5 x 7 = 35

Carry the 3.

1000	100	10	1
		6 (carried 3, 2 crossed out)	7
	x	5	3
	2	0	1
		5	0

Multiply tens by tens.

5 x 6 = 30 + 3 = 33

1000	100	10	1
		6 (carried 3, 2 crossed out)	7
	x	5	3
	2	0	1
3	3	5	0

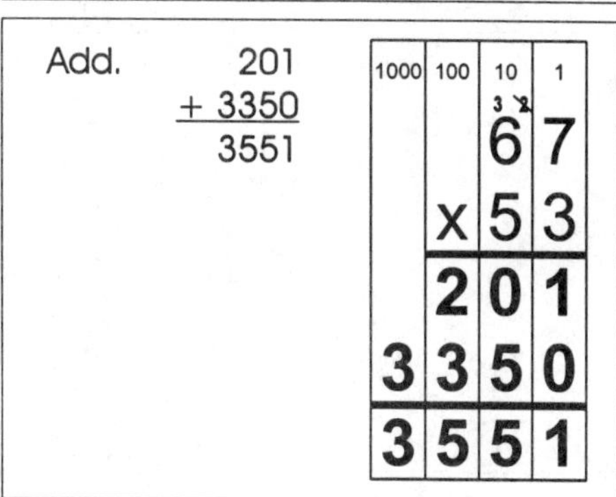

Add. 201
+ 3350
3551

1000	100	10	1
		6 (carried 3, 2 crossed out)	7
	x	5	3
	2	0	1
3	3	5	0
3	5	5	1

75
x 34
300
2250

47
x 36
282
0

94
x 37

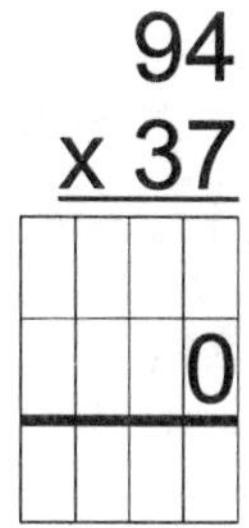

0

36
x 84

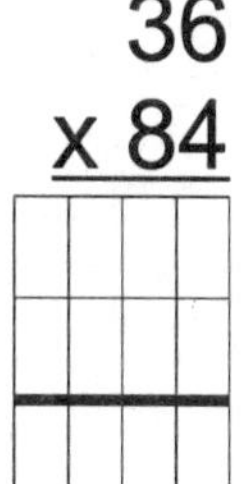

62
x 97

39
x 53

83
x 74

48
x 63

74
x 95

46
x 38

Multiplying
2 digits by 2 digits
Regrouping

Multiplication Practice

64 x 37	43 x 76	96 x 53	82 x 76	35 x 84
87 x 49	56 x 67	34 x 40	26 x 64	68 x 28
48 x 36	82 x 96	76 x 64	57 x 72	95 x 48
63 x 97	78 x 34	46 x 82	65 x 43	79 x 47
84 x 69	69 x 46	33 x 68	22 x 98	39 x 85

Multiplying
3 digits by 2 digits
Regrouping

Multiplication Practice

Example

384 x 46 2304	384 x 46 2304 0	384 x 46 2304 15360	384 x 46 2304 15360 17,664
Multiply by ones.	Put a 0 in the ones column.	Multiply by tens.	Add.

576 x 42	368 x 84	667 x 56	738 x 68	367 x 74
668 x 37	490 x 63	796 x 82	258 x 76	783 x 47
738 x 48	457 x 63	804 x 76	746 x 34	248 x 83

Multiplying
3 digits by 2 digits
Regrouping

Multiplication Practice

437 x 64	576 x 43	253 x 96	476 x 82	684 x 35
249 x 87	867 x 56	748 x 34	264 x 36	328 x 68
736 x 48	496 x 82	304 x 76	572 x 57	348 x 95
497 x 63	934 x 70	782 x 47	843 x 65	447 x 79
369 x 84	746 x 69	668 x 33	798 x 22	405 x 39

Multiplying
3 digits by 3 digits
Regrouping

Multiplication Practice

Example

768 x 432 1536 Multiply by ones.	768 x 432 1536 0 Put a 0 in the ones column.	768 x 432 1536 23040 Multiply by tens.
768 x 432 1536 23040 00 Put 0's in the ones and tens columns.	768 x 432 1536 23040 307200 Multiply by hundreds.	768 x 432 1536 23040 307200 331,776 Add.

479 x 643	638 x 549	796 x 463	567 x 926
868 x 435	368 x 307	247 x 969	406 x 783

Multiplying
3 digits by 3 digits
Regrouping

Multiplication Practice

473 x 464	567 x 843	302 x 696	679 x 282
942 x 587	768 x 206	578 x 434	646 x 636
630 x 848	896 x 982	436 x 676	275 x 757
794 x 563	934 x 478	875 x 807	348 x 965
967 x 384	604 x 469	855 x 633	798 x 522

Multiplication Practice

73 x 64	420 x 43	639 x 287	500 x 500
92 x 57	256 x 729	999 x 999	46 x 36
123 x 201	86 x 92	437 x 606	757 x 259
79 x 56	834 x 378	805 x 807	48 x 65
429 x 503	74 x 69	55 x 33	100 x 100

Multiplication Practice

227 x 918	67 x 43	30 x 60	479 x 283
803 x 478	78 x 26	508 x 34	946 x 637
721 x 48	396 x 907	36 x 74	200 x 557
79 x 63	93 x 48	475 x 347	748 x 865
900 x 300	964 x 459	843 x 643	82 x 98

Multiplication Practice

234 x 432	57 x 83	352 x 96	609 x 282
42 x 87	643 x 206	57 x 43	600 x 502
27 x 43	896 x 982	43 x 66	572 x 457
802 x 53	834 x 400	700 x 647	34 x 65
463 x 84	604 x 369	85 x 63	408 x 502

Multiplication Practice

62 x 79	507 x 437	35 x 96	437 x 364
92 x 87	852 x 56	964 x 34	703 x 61
80 x 70	698 x 389	600 x 438	572 x 48
563 x 721	309 x 807	75 x 87	400 x 206
97 x 34	604 x 49	558 x 339	897 x 502

Answers
Pages 4 - 7

Multiplication Practice

Page 4

1 x2 2	2 x2 4	3 x0 0	0 x1 0	4 x3 12	2 x0 0
2 x3 6	6 x0 0	8 x4 32	1 x4 4	9 x0 0	4 x2 8
5 x0 0	2 x1 2	7 x4 28	4 x0 0	6 x4 24	0 x0 0
0 x3 0	6 x2 12	3 x2 6	3 x1 3	7 x0 0	5 x1 5
4 x1 4	9 x4 36	9 x1 9	1 x0 0	9 x3 27	9 x2 18
4 x4 16	8 x2 16	8 x3 24	2 x4 8	1 x1 1	5 x2 10
8 x0 0	3 x3 9	6 x1 6	3 x4 12	7 x1 7	6 x3 18
1 x3 3	5 x3 15	5 x4 20	8 x1 8	0 x2 0	7 x2 14
7 x3 21	0 x4 0				

Page 5

9 x5 45	0 x5 0	8 x7 56	5 x9 45	2 x8 16	7 x6 42
3 x5 15	4 x9 36	4 x7 28	1 x8 8	4 x5 20	0 x8 0
3 x6 18	2 x7 14	1 x9 9	7 x5 35	9 x8 72	5 x8 40
9 x9 81	1 x7 7	6 x9 54	1 x5 5	0 x6 0	9 x7 63
5 x5 25	7 x7 49	3 x9 27	4 x6 24	5 x6 30	6 x8 48
8 x9 72	1 x6 6	3 x7 21	8 x8 64	5 x7 35	2 x9 18
0 x7 0	7 x8 56	0 x9 0	6 x6 36	4 x8 32	6 x5 30
7 x9 63	9 x6 54	8 x6 48	2 x6 12	3 x8 24	6 x7 42
2 x5 10	8 x5 40				

Page 6

13 x 2 26	20 x 3 60	11 x 9 99	41 x 2 82	13 x 3 39
57 x 7 399	25 x 9 225	36 x 2 72	48 x 5 240	22 x 9 198
33 x 2 66	69 x 1 69	10 x 8 80	65 x 1 65	41 x 2 82
352 x 8 2,816	176 x 5 880	306 x 4 1,224	280 x 7 1,960	917 x 6 5,502
33 x 9 297	46 x 8 368	69 x 2 138	65 x 3 195	87 x 2 174
79 x 4 316	59 x 3 177	38 x 2 76	77 x 5 385	12 x 9 108
637 x 7 4,459	422 x 4 1,688	380 x 4 1,520	996 x 6 5,976	245 x 3 735
880 x 4 3,520	406 x 8 3,248	180 x 7 1,260	104 x 3 312	409 x 7 2,863

Page 7

23 x 21 483	21 x 34 714	42 x 12 504	19 x 11 209
92 x 57 5,244	78 x 20 1,560	50 x 44 2,200	66 x 66 4,356
37 x 40 1,480	96 x 82 7,872	30 x 76 2,280	75 x 57 4,275
497 x 653 324,541	934 x 478 446,452	847 x 875 741,125	348 x 956 332,688
906 x 324 293,544	229 x 409 93,661	850 x 630 535,500	708 x 520 368,160

Answers
Pages 8 - 11

Multiplication Practice

Page 8

Example 32 x 3

Multiply ones by ones. (10 | 1: 3 2 / x 3 / 6)

Multiply tens by ones. (10 | 1: 3 2 / x 3 / 9 6)

12 x 4 48	11 x 6 66	41 x 2 82	23 x 3 69	30 x 2 60
11 x 9 99	13 x 3 39	30 x 3 90	22 x 4 88	44 x 2 88
77 x 1 77	10 x 8 80	43 x 2 86	31 x 3 93	12 x 3 36
22 x 2 44	14 x 2 28	90 x 1 90	11 x 8 88	49 x 1 49
19 x 1 19	27 x 1 27	11 x 4 44	13 x 2 26	65 x 1 65
34 x 2 68	21 x 4 84	32 x 2 64	99 x 1 99	10 x 9 90

Page 9

11 x 6 66	89 x 1 89	34 x 2 68	22 x 4 88	13 x 3 39
13 x 2 26	10 x 9 90	32 x 2 64	38 x 1 38	10 x 5 50
98 x 1 98	41 x 2 82	22 x 3 66	11 x 3 33	23 x 3 69
12 x 4 48	10 x 5 50	11 x 4 44	28 x 1 28	10 x 6 60
33 x 2 66	10 x 8 80	69 x 1 69	65 x 1 65	10 x 2 20
79 x 1 79	12 x 3 36	34 x 2 68	11 x 5 55	12 x 2 24
31 x 3 93	10 x 7 70	21 x 4 84	10 x 6 60	23 x 3 69
11 x 7 77	41 x 2 82	18 x 1 18	11 x 8 88	49 x 1 49

Page 10

Example 83 x 4

Multiply ones by ones. 4 x 3 = 12 Carry the 1. (100 | 10 | 1: 1 / 8 3 / x 4 / 2)

Multiply tens by ones. 4 x 8 = 32 + 1 = 33 (100 | 10 | 1: 1 / 8 3 / x 4 / 3 3 2)

13 x 4 52	18 x 6 108	46 x 2 92	29 x 3 87	16 x 4 64
22 x 9 198	25 x 3 75	64 x 3 192	75 x 5 375	76 x 9 684
27 x 5 135	99 x 8 792	43 x 6 258	44 x 4 176	82 x 5 410
19 x 5 95	14 x 6 84	93 x 4 372	63 x 8 504	49 x 7 343
18 x 4 72	27 x 5 135	35 x 4 140	15 x 9 135	12 x 8 96
34 x 6 204	27 x 3 81	38 x 2 76	99 x 2 198	82 x 9 738

Page 11

19 x 6 114	89 x 3 267	34 x 5 170	88 x 8 704	13 x 9 117
67 x 7 469	15 x 9 135	36 x 2 72	38 x 5 190	22 x 9 198
98 x 7 686	44 x 8 352	27 x 4 108	84 x 6 504	25 x 3 75
52 x 8 416	16 x 5 80	36 x 4 144	28 x 7 196	17 x 6 102
33 x 9 297	46 x 8 368	69 x 2 138	65 x 3 195	87 x 2 174
79 x 4 316	59 x 3 177	38 x 2 76	77 x 5 385	12 x 9 108
37 x 7 259	46 x 4 184	38 x 4 152	99 x 6 594	24 x 3 72
88 x 4 352	46 x 8 368	18 x 7 126	14 x 3 42	49 x 7 343

Answers
Pages 12 - 15

Multiplication Practice

Page 12

Example

Step	1000	100	10	1
Multiply ones by ones. 4 x 3 = 12 Carry the 1.		3	8 (carry 1)	3
			x	4
				2

Step	1000	100	10	1
Multiply tens by ones. 4 x 8 = 32 + 1 = 33 Carry the 3.		3 (carry 3)	8 (carry 1)	3
			x	4
			3	2

Step	1000	100	10	1
Multiply hundreds by ones. 4 x 3 = 12 + 3 = 15		3 (carry 3)	8	3
			x	4
	1	5	3	2

114	517	706	529	317
x 4	x 6	x 2	x 3	x 4
456	3,102	1,412	1,587	1,268
623	426	164	275	674
x 9	x 3	x 3	x 5	x 9
5,607	1,278	492	1,375	6,066
327	299	840	444	882
x 5	x 8	x 6	x 4	x 5
1,635	2,392	5,040	1,776	4,410
419	814	793	263	249
x 5	x 6	x 4	x 8	x 7
2,095	4,884	3,172	2,104	1,743
118	207	935	515	612
x 4	x 4	x 4	x 9	x 8
472	828	3,740	4,635	4,896
434	727	608	999	883
x 5	x 3	x 2	x 3	x 9
2,170	2,181	1,216	2,997	7,947

Page 13

317	288	324	848	273
x 7	x 2	x 5	x 8	x 9
2,219	576	1,620	6,784	2,457
464	205	736	308	222
x 8	x 9	x 2	x 5	x 9
3,712	1,845	1,472	1,540	1,998
598	844	237	884	285
x 7	x 3	x 6	x 5	x 3
4,186	2,532	1,422	4,420	855
152	196	370	238	367
x 6	x 5	x 4	x 7	x 6
912	980	1,480	1,666	2,202
333	505	689	657	827
x 5	x 4	x 2	x 3	x 4
1,665	2,020	1,378	1,971	3,308
472	959	538	727	123
x 4	x 3	x 5	x 5	x 9
1,888	2,877	2,690	3,635	1,107
437	642	358	969	249
x 7	x 4	x 6	x 6	x 8
3,059	2,568	2,148	5,814	1,992
188	746	918	814	409
x 4	x 8	x 7	x 3	x 7
752	5,968	6,426	2,442	2,863

Page 14

32	13	88	114	884
x 2	x 4	x 9	x 4	x 5
64	52	792	456	4,420
238	22	18	79	515
x 7	x 4	x 6	x 4	x 9
1,666	88	108	316	4,635
196	41	605	49	426
x 5	x 8	x 2	x 2	x 8
980	328	1,210	98	3,408
65	874	31	273	80
x 3	x 9	x 8	x 3	x 9
195	7,866	248	819	720
745	15	777	421	33
x 6	x 8	x 7	x 5	x 2
4,470	120	5,439	2,105	66
79	19	364	76	967
x 2	x 3	x 2	x 4	x 7
158	57	728	304	6,769
368	66	291	600	293
x 3	x 7	x 4	x 6	x 4
1,104	462	1,164	3,600	1,172
76	404	18	198	479
x 7	x 4	x 7	x 8	x 2
532	1,616	126	1,584	958

Page 15

Example

	1000	100	10	1
			3	2
		x	2	1
			3	2

Multiply by ones.
1 x 32 = 32

	1000	100	10	1
			3	2
		x	2	1
			3	2
				0

Put a zero in the ones column.

	1000	100	10	1
			3	2
		x	2	1
			3	2
		6	4	0

Multiply by tens.
2 x 32 = 64

	1000	100	10	1
			3	2
		x	2	1
			3	2
		6	4	0
		6	7	2

Add.
32 + 640 = 672

12	22	12	11	43
x 14	x 44	x 42	x 65	x 21
48	88	24	55	43
120	880	480	660	860
168	968	504	715	903
21	13	31	23	56
x 23	x 20	x 21	x 32	x 11
483	260	651	736	616
23	33	90	34	13
x 31	x 13	x 11	x 21	x 33
713	429	990	714	429

Answers
Pages 16 - 19

Multiplication Practice

Page 16

14 x 12 168	13 x 33 429	32 x 23 736	12 x 14 168	32 x 12 384
23 x 21 483	42 x 12 504	21 x 30 630	23 x 21 483	12 x 42 504
31 x 23 713	12 x 31 372	43 x 21 903	23 x 32 736	30 x 21 630
44 x 22 968	11 x 78 858	47 x 11 517	21 x 43 903	19 x 11 209
13 x 22 286	60 x 11 660	33 x 13 429	22 x 14 308	11 x 80 880

Page 17

Example

Multiply ones by ones. 3 x 7 = 21 Carry the 2. 1000 100 10 1 67 x 53 1	Multiply tens by ones. 3 x 6=18+2=20 1000 100 10 1 67 x 53 201	Put a zero in the ones column. 1000 100 10 1 67 x 53 201 0
Multiply ones by tens. 5 x 7 = 35 Carry the 3. 1000 100 10 1 67 x 53 201 50	Multiply tens by tens. 5 x 6=30+3=33 1000 100 10 1 67 x 53 201 3350	Add. 201 + 3350 3551 1000 100 10 1 67 x 53 201 3350 3551

75 x 34 300 2250 2550	47 x 36 282 1410 1692	94 x 37 658 2820 3478	36 x 84 144 2880 3024	62 x 97 434 5580 6014
39 x 53 2,067	83 x 74 6,142	48 x 63 3,024	74 x 95 7,030	46 x 38 1,748

Page 18

64 x 37 2,368	43 x 76 3,268	96 x 53 5,088	82 x 76 6,232	35 x 84 2,940
87 x 49 4,263	56 x 67 3,752	34 x 40 1,360	26 x 64 1,664	68 x 28 1,904
48 x 36 1,728	82 x 96 7,872	76 x 64 4,864	57 x 72 4,104	95 x 48 4,560
63 x 97 6,111	78 x 34 2,652	46 x 82 3,772	65 x 43 2,795	79 x 47 3,713
84 x 69 5,796	69 x 46 3,174	33 x 68 2,244	22 x 98 2,156	39 x 85 3,315

Page 19

Example

384 x 46 2304 Multiply by ones.	384 x 46 2304 0 Put a 0 in the ones column.	384 x 46 2304 15360 Multiply by tens.	384 x 46 2304 15360 17,664 Add.

576 x 42 24,192	368 x 84 30,912	667 x 56 37,352	738 x 68 50,184	367 x 74 27,158
668 x 37 24,716	490 x 63 30,870	796 x 82 65,272	258 x 76 19,608	783 x 47 36,801
738 x 48 35,424	457 x 63 28,791	804 x 76 61,104	746 x 34 25,364	248 x 83 20,584

Answers
Pages 20 - 23

Multiplication Practice

Page 20

437	576	253	476	684
x 64	x 43	x 96	x 82	x 35
27,968	24,768	24,288	39,032	23,940
249	867	748	264	328
x 87	x 56	x 34	x 36	x 68
21,663	48,552	25,432	9,504	22,304
736	496	304	572	348
x 48	x 82	x 76	x 57	x 95
35,328	40,672	23,104	32,604	33,060
497	934	782	843	447
x 63	x 70	x 47	x 65	x 79
31,311	65,380	36,754	54,795	35,313
369	746	668	798	405
x 84	x 69	x 33	x 22	x 39
30,996	51,474	22,044	17,556	15,795

Page 21

Example

768 x 432 1536 Multiply by ones.	768 x 432 1536 0 Put a 0 in the ones column.	768 x 432 1536 23040 Multiply by tens.
768 x 432 1536 23040 00 Put 0's in the ones and tens columns.	768 x 432 1536 23040 307200 Multiply by hundreds.	768 x 432 1536 23040 307200 331,776 Add.

479	638	796	567
x 643	x 549	x 463	x 926
307,997	350,262	368,548	525,042
868	368	247	406
x 435	x 307	x 969	x 783
377,580	112,976	239,343	317,898

Page 22

473	567	302	679
x 464	x 843	x 696	x 282
219,472	477,981	210,192	191,478
942	768	578	646
x 587	x 206	x 434	x 636
552,954	158,208	250,852	410,856
630	896	436	275
x 848	x 982	x 676	x 757
534,240	879,872	294,736	208,175
794	934	875	348
x 563	x 478	x 807	x 965
447,022	446,452	706,125	335,820
967	604	855	798
x 384	x 469	x 633	x 522
371,328	283,276	541,215	416,556

Page 23

73	420	639	500
x 64	x 43	x 287	x 500
4,672	18,060	183,393	250,000
92	256	999	46
x 57	x 729	x 999	x 36
5,244	186,624	998,001	1,656
123	86	437	757
x 201	x 92	x 606	x 259
24,723	7,912	264,822	196,063
79	834	805	48
x 56	x 378	x 807	x 65
4,424	315,252	649,635	3,120
429	74	55	100
x 503	x 69	x 33	x 100
215,787	5,106	1,815	10,000

Answers
Pages 24 - 26

Multiplication Practice

Page 24

227 x 918 208,386	67 x 43 2,881	30 x 60 1,800	479 x 283 135,557
803 x 478 383,834	78 x 26 2,028	508 x 34 17,272	946 x 637 602,602
721 x 48 34,608	396 x 907 359,172	36 x 74 2,664	200 x 557 111,400
79 x 63 4,977	93 x 48 4,464	475 x 347 164,825	748 x 865 647,020
900 x 300 270,000	964 x 459 442,476	843 x 643 542,049	82 x 98 8,036

Page 25

234 x 432 101,088	57 x 83 4,731	352 x 96 33,792	609 x 282 171,738
42 x 87 3,654	643 x 206 132,458	57 x 43 2,451	600 x 502 301,200
27 x 43 1,161	896 x 982 879,872	43 x 66 2,838	572 x 457 261,404
802 x 53 42,506	834 x 400 333,600	700 x 647 452,900	34 x 65 2,210
463 x 84 38,892	604 x 369 222,876	85 x 63 5,355	408 x 502 204,816

Page 26

62 x 79 4,898	507 x 437 221,559	35 x 96 3,360	437 x 364 159,068
92 x 87 8004	852 x 56 47,712	964 x 34 32,776	703 x 61 42,883
80 x 70 5,600	698 x 389 271,522	600 x 438 262,800	572 x 48 27,456
563 x 721 405,923	309 x 807 249,363	75 x 87 6,525	400 x 206 82,400
97 x 34 3,298	604 x 49 29,596	558 x 339 189,162	897 x 502 450,294